The Playroom

One Monday morning a letter came for Mum and Dad. 'It's from Great-grandfather,' said Mum. 'It's his birthday on Saturday and he wants us to go and spend the weekend with him.'

'Good,' said Dad. 'I was going to decorate the kitchen this weekend. A visit to North Wales will be far more fun.'

Jo hadn't been to her Great-grandfather's house since she was a baby. She could hardly believe her eyes when they drove through the gates. The huge building looked more like a castle than a home.

'Wow!' she gasped. 'It's amazing. Do you think Great-grandfather will remember me? I won't know what to say to him.'

'Of course, he'll remember you,' said Mum.

Great-grandfather was waiting to meet them at the front door. Jo knew as soon as she saw him that they were going to be great friends.

'Come in, come in!' he said. 'I haven't seen you since you were a baby, Jo, so we'll have a lot to talk about.'

After tea Great-grandfather showed Jo around the house. There was a lot to see. 'It's very easy to get lost in this place,' he said, 'but you'll soon get used to it. There is one special room that I want you to see, and here it is.' As the door opened, Jo gasped. 'It's like a toy shop,' she said.

'Almost,' laughed Great-grandfather. 'It's the playroom. Let's go and see what we can find.'

'You may not believe this,' said Great-grandfather, 'but I was once your age. This was where I spent my happiest times.'

'Are these all your toys?' asked Jo.

'Not all of them,' said Great-grandfather. 'Some were my grandfather's, some were my father's, and some were your father's.'

'They're wonderful!' gasped Jo. 'Do you still play with them?'

'Every day,' replied Great-grandfather.

'Do you have a favourite?' asked Jo.

'Oh yes,' said Great-grandfather, 'come and see.'

In the far corner of the room was a toy castle. It was the biggest castle that Jo had ever seen. 'My father made this for me, when I was about your age,' said Great-grandfather. 'I used to sit here for hours and make up stories about knights and dragons.'

'Will you tell me one?' asked Jo.

'Of course,' said Great-grandfather.

‘I used to pretend that I was the lord of this castle,’ he said. ‘I was held prisoner in this tower by the wicked Red Baron and his men. My friends the white knights wanted to storm the castle and rescue me but they couldn’t think of a way to do it.’

‘Did you ever escape?’ asked Jo.

‘No, I’m still in the tower,’ laughed Great-grandfather, ‘but once a year, on my birthday, the white knights and the red ones come to life and fight a great battle. One day the white knights may win. Come on, Jo, time for supper.’

Jo's bedroom was next to the playroom. After supper she climbed into bed. She was almost asleep when she heard a terrific noise. Trumpets were blowing, horses were neighing and people were shouting and cheering. Jo got out of bed and went to investigate.

The playroom glowed with a mysterious white light. It seemed magical but real at the same time. A pale mist hung over the toy castle, but the strangest thing of all was that Jo was no bigger than a toy soldier. She gazed up in amazement at the tall towers of the castle which seemed to touch the sky. 'What's happened to me?' she gasped.

Suddenly one of the white knights spotted Jo. He turned his horse and galloped towards her. 'Come with me,' he cried. 'You are in great danger. The red knights are everywhere.'

'But who are you?' asked Jo.

'I am Sir Edmund, leader of the white knights. Today we must try to rescue the prisoner in the tower.'

Sir Edmund lifted Jo on to his horse and they galloped across the carpet towards the white knights' tents. Some of the white knights came to greet Jo.

'How are you going to get into the castle?' she asked. 'Have you got a plan?'

'Well not exactly,' said Edmund. 'We try every year and every year we fail. The castle is too strong for us.'

'Then we'll just have to trick our way in,' said Jo. 'I think I've got an idea. First we shall need a disguise.'

On the floor was a box of paints. ‘This is just what we want,’ said Jo. ‘Does anybody know where there’s a paintbrush?’

‘I do,’ said one of the knights. ‘I’ll go and get it if somebody will help me carry it.’

‘The next thing we need,’ said Jo, ‘is the clockwork train and the rails that go with it.’

‘What are you going to do?’ asked Edmund.

‘First of all,’ said Jo, ‘we’re going to paint you red. That will be your disguise.’

The red knights, who were guarding the gate, were having their dinner. They saw Edmund, in his new disguise, bringing Jo towards them.

'Who have you got there?' said one of the guards.

'I've got another prisoner to put in the tower,' said Edmund. 'Open the gate and let us in.'
The gate creaked open and Jo and Edmund stepped inside the castle.

'It worked,' whispered Jo.

Jo and Edmund walked nervously across the courtyard. It was beginning to rain. As they reached the door of the tower it opened and the Red Baron himself came out. 'What have we here?' he demanded.
Edmund explained that Jo was his prisoner and that he was going to have her locked in the tower. At first the Red Baron looked pleased. Then he began to frown. The rain had started to wash off Edmund's disguise.

The Red Baron let out a cry of rage. Jo dived down behind his legs and Edmund, who was now a streaky pink colour, pushed him over.

'Quick!' said Jo. 'We have to get into the tower.'

They rushed through the door and began to run up the stairs taking them two at a time.

At the very top of the stairs was a door with a key in it. Jo could hear the Red Baron and his men thundering up the stairs behind them.

'In here,' shouted Edmund.

They burst into the tower.

'Quick! Lock the door,' gasped Jo. 'That should keep them out for a few minutes.'

Edmund turned the key in the lock just in time. The Red Baron and his men began to hammer on the door.

'We're trapped,' said Jo.

'I've been trapped in here for years,' said a voice from the darkness.

'Great-grandfather!' gasped Jo. 'What are you doing here?'

'I told you I've been a prisoner here for years and years,' said Great-grandfather.

'Oh dear,' said Jo. 'I was trying to rescue you but now we're all caught. Is there really no other way out of this room?'

'Only on to the roof,' said Great-grandfather. 'That's where I take my exercise. But there's no way down.'

'The roof! That's it!' said Jo. 'I think we might have a chance.'

They climbed through the trap-door. On the roof was a toy aeroplane. 'I knew it,' shouted Jo. 'I remember seeing it land here.'

At that moment there was a terrific crash as the Red Baron and his men broke into the tower.

'Quick!' said Jo. 'It's our only chance.'

Edmund pushed the toy aeroplane to the edge of the roof and Jo helped Great-grandfather climb aboard.

Just as the Red Baron grabbed the tail of the aeroplane it slipped over the edge and began to float gently towards the ground. 'Help!' yelled the Baron, who forgot to let go.

Just before the plane landed the Red Baron lost his grip.

'Bombs away!' laughed Great-grandfather. There was a huge splash as the Baron fell into the moat. The white knights pulled him out. Great-grandfather frowned at the Red Baron. 'For many years I have been your prisoner,' he said. 'Now you are mine. Will you make peace and surrender the castle?'

'Never!' said the Red Baron, brushing a frog from his shoulder.

'Then we shall take it by force,' said Jo.

While Jo and Edmund had been away in the castle the other white knights had laid the tracks of the clockwork train up to the castle gate.
Great-grandfather and the white knights climbed aboard the train. Jo and Edmund wound up the clockwork. Then they jumped on to the engine and Jo released the brake. The train moved along the track and began to gather speed.
With a great bang the train crashed through the castle gate. The white knights gave a mighty roar, jumped from the carriages, and drove the red knights from the castle.

'We've won! We've won!' shouted Jo.

'It's all thanks to you,' said Great-grandfather.

'Kneel down, Jo,' said Edmund. Jo did as she was told. Edmund touched her lightly on each shoulder with his sword. The trumpets sounded and the white knights clashed their swords on their shields and cheered. 'Three cheers for Jo, the bravest knight of all,' they shouted.

Jo said goodbye to all her friends and she and Great-grandfather walked out of the playroom and out of their great adventure.

When Jo woke up the next morning she went straight into the playroom. Everything was as she had seen it the day before. The red knights were back in the castle and the white ones were outside. There were no signs of her adventure.

'Good morning,' said Great-grandfather. 'I hope you slept well.'

'I did,' said Jo, 'but I had a very strange dream.'

'Are you sure it was a dream?' smiled Great-grandfather.

Castles

In many parts of Britain you can see the remains of hill forts. Hill forts were the first British castles. They were built by the Celts, who lived in Britain over two thousand years ago. A tribe would build its village on top of a hill and dig deep ditches around it. This would protect them from their enemies. The ditches were so huge that they can still be seen today.

Two thousand years ago Britain was invaded by people called the Romans. Their soldiers lived in huge army camps, and they built strong walls as well as ditches.

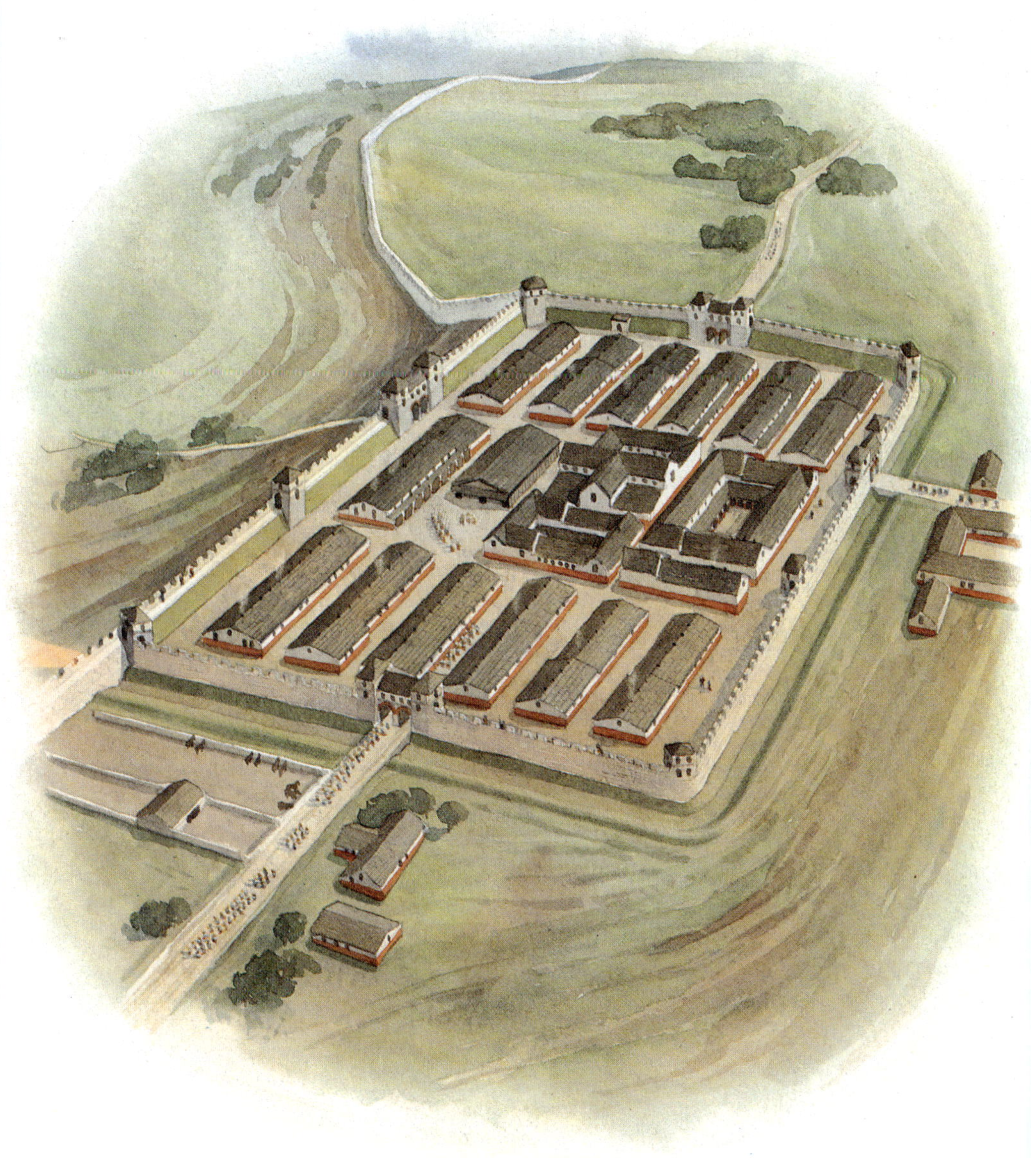

About a thousand years ago England was invaded by the Normans, who came from Northern France. They built a type of castle called a Motte and Bailey. A strong wooden tower was put up on top of a huge mound. This was the Motte. It was used as a look-out tower to spot the enemy. The Bailey was an area protected by wooden walls and ditches. This is where people lived, stored their food, and kept their animals.

When the Normans had conquered England they began to build stronger castles of stone.
Look at this picture of a castle. It is more like a small town than a home. If a castle was attacked by an enemy army the people inside would need enough food and water to last several weeks.
There were many ways of attacking a castle.
Some castles were so strong that an enemy had to camp outside the walls and wait for the people inside to run out of food and water.
This was called a siege.
People stopped building castles when gunpowder was invented. Even the strongest walls could be knocked down by big guns.

The ghostly battle

On the top of Wandlebury Hill, near Cambridge, are the ruins of an old fort. Some people keep away from Wandlebury Hill. They believe it is haunted by the ancient warriors who lived in the time of King Arthur and his knights.

There is a legend which says that if anyone is brave enough to ride into the ruined fort at midnight and blow three times on his bugle a ghostly warrior will appear in front of him ready to do battle.

One bitter winter's evening, many hundreds of years ago, a famous knight, Sir Osbert, came to stay in his friend's castle. The castle lay at the foot of Wandlebury Hill.

Sir Osbert's friend made him welcome, and provided a great feast for him.

When they had eaten, the two friends sat in front of the brightly burning fire. They began to tell each other stories whilst the people of the castle listened in wonder. At last, Sir Osbert's friend told the legend of the haunted hill.

Now, Sir Osbert was a brave and noble knight. He rose from his stool with a laugh and called for his armour. 'I will accept this challenge,' he said. 'I will try my skill against this ghostly champion, and I will try it tonight.'

A little before midnight, the brave knight rode out of the castle gate. The iron-shod hooves of his horse struck sparks from the cobbled road. By the light of a bright full moon the people of the castle watched him ride up the icy path to Wandlebury Hill.

Sir Osbert urged his horse through the gap that had once been the gate of the old fort and found himself on a flat and frosty field. Trembling with excitement he put the bugle to his cold lips and blew the first blast. The shrill note echoed around the empty hills. At the second blast Sir Osbert thought he heard the snorting of a war horse. At the third blast the ghostly warrior appeared before him mounted on a huge, silver horse.

At once the mysterious rider came galloping across the field towards Sir Osbert. The stranger's lance grazed Sir Osbert's leg but Osbert was ready for him. His own lance struck the breast of the ghostly warrior and flung him to the ground.

Sir Osbert seized the bridle of the silver horse. But though he searched every inch of the ruined fort there was no sign of the ghostly warrior.

Sir Osbert rode back to his friend's castle and everybody rushed forward to welcome him. They looked in amazement at the magnificent silver steed that walked quietly behind him.

All through the night the silver steed stood quietly in the castle stables, guarded by Sir Osbert's squire. But as the dawn began to break the horse stamped its hoof on the stable floor, shook its flowing mane, snorted three times, and plunged and reared until it broke free. Before anyone could stop it, the horse was galloping back up the frosty path to the ruined fort.

Sir Osbert and his friends gazed in wonder as the horse rose from the top of the hill into the mists of the morning sky. Since that day nobody has seen or heard of the ghostly warrior, nor his silver steed. Since that day nobody has dared accept the challenge of Wandlebury Hill.